INDULGENCE

# cupcakes

39 irresistible sweet treat recipes

MURDOCH BOOKS

# Contents

If you are using silicone moulds in place of muffin tins and paper cases, for the best result, grease the insides of the moulds very lightly with vegetable oil or butter so that the cooked cupcakes are easily turned out. For ease of handling, place the filled moulds on a baking tray before they go in the oven.

# Family favourites

From naughty to nice, this delicious assortment will bring out the child in all of us.

# Orange poppy seed cupcakes

**MAKES 15**

40 g (1½ oz/¼ cup) poppy seeds,
plus extra to sprinkle
125 ml (4 fl oz/½ cup) warm milk
150 g (5½ oz) unsalted butter, softened
3 teaspoons finely grated orange zest
170 g (6 oz/¾ cup) caster (superfine) sugar
2 eggs
185 g (6½ oz/1½ cups) self-raising flour, sifted

**Citrus icing (frosting)**
250 g (9 oz) unsalted butter, softened
375 g (13 oz/3 cups) icing (confectioners')
sugar, sifted
3 teaspoons finely grated orange zest

Preheat the oven to 180°C (350°F/Gas 4). Line 15 standard muffin holes with paper cases.

Combine the poppy seeds and milk in a bowl and set aside for at least 15 minutes.

Place the butter, orange zest, caster sugar, eggs and flour in a large bowl. Add the poppy seed mixture and beat with electric beaters on low speed until combined. Increase to a medium speed and beat for 3 minutes, or until the mixture is thick and pale.

Divide the mixture evenly among the cases. Bake for 15 minutes, or until a skewer comes out clean when inserted into the centre of a cake. Transfer onto a wire rack to cool.

To make the citrus icing, place the butter, icing sugar and zest in a large bowl and beat with electric beaters until light and fluffy. Spread the icing over the cakes and sprinkle with the extra poppy seeds.

6

# Plum crumble
# patty cakes

Preheat the oven to 180°C (350°F/Gas 4). Line 24 flat-bottomed patty holes with paper cases.

Cream the butter, sugar and vanilla with electric beaters until light and creamy. Add the eggs one at a time, beating well after each addition. Sift the flours together and fold in alternately with the plum juice. Divide the mixture evenly among the cases and cover each with slices of plum.

To make the crumble topping, place the sugar, flour and butter in a bowl. Mix together with your fingertips until it resembles coarse breadcrumbs. Sprinkle the crumble over each cake, covering the plums.

Bake for 15–18 minutes, or until golden. Transfer onto a wire rack to cool.

**MAKES 24**

185 g (6½ oz) unsalted butter, softened
170 g (6 oz/¾ cup) caster (superfine) sugar
1 teaspoon natural vanilla extract
3 eggs
125 g (4½ oz/1 cup) self-raising flour
30 g (1 oz/¼ cup) plain (all-purpose) flour
125 ml (4 fl oz/½ cup) tinned natural plum juice
9 tinned plums in natural juice, stones removed,
  thinly sliced

**Crumble topping**
110 g (3¾ oz/½ cup) raw (demerara) sugar
125 g (4½ oz/1 cup) plain (all-purpose) flour
100 g (3½ oz) unsalted butter, chilled and diced

# Gingerbread cupcakes

**MAKES 16**

250 g (9 oz/2 cups) self-raising flour
90 g (3¼ oz/¾ cup) plain (all-purpose) flour
½ teaspoon bicarbonate of soda (baking soda)
3 teaspoons ground ginger
1 teaspoon ground cinnamon
1 teaspoon mixed spice
230 g (8½ oz/1 cup) soft brown sugar
55 g (2 oz/¼ cup) glacé ginger, chopped
235 g (8½ oz/⅔ cup) golden syrup or maple syrup
100 g (3½ oz) unsalted butter, chopped
250 ml (9 fl oz/1 cup) buttermilk
2 eggs, lightly beaten

**Ginger icing (frosting)**
250 g (9 oz/2 cups) icing (confectioners') sugar, sifted
1 teaspoon ground ginger
20 g (¾ oz) unsalted butter, softened

Preheat the oven to 200°C (400°F/Gas 6). Line 16 standard muffin holes with paper cases.

Sift the flours, bicarbonate of soda, ground ginger, cinnamon and mixed spice into a large bowl. Stir in the brown sugar and glacé ginger. Make a well in the centre.

Put the golden syrup and butter in a small saucepan and stir over medium heat until melted. Remove from the heat and cool. Combine the syrup mixture, the buttermilk and egg in a jug, mix together and pour into the well in the dry ingredients. Fold in gently until just combined — the batter should be lumpy.

Divide the mixture evenly among the cases. Bake for 20–25 minutes, or until a skewer comes out clean when inserted into the centre of a cake. Transfer onto a wire rack to cool.

To make the ginger icing, place the icing sugar, ginger and butter in a small heatproof bowl. Stir in enough warm water to form a smooth paste. Sit the bowl over a saucepan of simmering water, making sure the bowl doesn't touch the water, and stir until smooth and glossy. Remove from the heat. Spread 2 teaspoons of icing over each cake. Sprinkle with icing sugar.

# Hot cross bun cakes

MAKES 12

250 g (9 oz/2 cups) self-raising flour
3 teaspoons ground cinnamon
125 g (4½ oz) unsalted butter, chopped
125 g (4½ oz/1 cup) sultanas (golden raisins)
45 g (1⅔ oz/¼ cup) mixed peel (mixed candied citrus peel)
170 g (6 oz/¾ cup) caster (superfine) sugar
185 ml (6 fl oz/¾ cup) milk
2 eggs, lightly beaten

**Glaze**
2 teaspoons powdered gelatine
2 tablespoons caster (superfine) sugar

**Icing (frosting)**
60 g (2¼ oz/½ cup) icing (confectioners') sugar
2 teaspoons lemon juice

Preheat the oven to 200°C (400°F/Gas 6). Grease 12 standard muffin holes.

Sift the flour and cinnamon into a large bowl, add the butter, then rub together with your fingertips until the mixture resembles fine breadcrumbs. Stir in the sultanas, mixed peel and caster sugar. Make a well in the centre.

Whisk the milk and egg in a jug, then pour into the well. Fold in gently until just combined — the batter should be lumpy.

Divide the mixture evenly among the muffin holes. Bake for 20–25 minutes, or until the cakes come away from the side of the tin. Cool briefly, then transfer onto a wire rack.

To make the glaze, combine the gelatine, caster sugar and 2 tablespoons of water in a small saucepan. Stir over low heat for 1 minute, or until the sugar and gelatine are dissolved. Remove from the heat. Brush the glaze over the warm cakes a couple of times, then allow them to cool.

To make the icing, mix the icing sugar and lemon juice together until smooth. Spoon the icing into a piping bag, and pipe a cross on each cake and allow them to set.

# Jaffa cupcakes

### MAKES 12

165 g (5¾ oz/1⅓ cups) self-raising flour
30 g (1 oz/¼ cup) unsweetened cocoa powder
220 g (7¾ oz/1 cup) caster (superfine) sugar
2 eggs, lightly beaten
170 ml (5½ fl oz/⅔ cup) milk
125 g (4½ oz/½ cup) unsalted butter, melted
1 tablespoon finely grated orange zest

#### Orange buttercream
250 g (9 oz/2 cups) icing (confectioners')
sugar, sifted
60 g (2¼ oz) unsalted butter, softened
2 teaspoons finely grated orange zest
2 tablespoons orange juice
orange cachous, to decorate

Preheat the oven to 180°C (350°F/Gas 4).
Line 12 standard muffin holes with paper cases.

Sift the flour and cocoa into a large bowl, then stir in the sugar. Add the egg, milk, melted butter and orange zest and beat with electric beaters for 2 minutes, or until well combined and smooth.

Divide the mixture evenly among the cases. Bake for 18–20 minutes, or until a skewer comes out clean when inserted into the centre of a cake. Transfer onto a wire rack to cool.

To make the orange buttercream, place 125 g (4½ oz/ 1 cup) of the icing sugar, the butter, zest and orange juice in a large mixing bowl. Beat with electric beaters until smooth and creamy. Gradually add the remaining icing sugar and beat until the cream is thick.

Decorate each cake with buttercream and orange cachous.

# Apricot, sour cream and coconut cupcakes

**MAKES 20**

220 g (7¾ oz/1¾ cups) self-raising flour
45 g (1⅔ oz/½ cup) desiccated coconut
125 g (4½ oz) unsalted butter
230 g (8½ oz/1 cup) caster (superfine) sugar
2 eggs, lightly beaten
250 ml (9 fl oz/1 cup) apricot nectar
125 g (4½ oz/½ cup) sour cream
825 g (1 lb 13 oz) tinned apricot halves in juice, drained (you need 20 apricot halves)
80 g (2¾ oz/¼ cup) apricot jam

Preheat the oven to 180°C (350°F/Gas 4). Line 20 standard muffin holes with paper cases.

Sift the flour into a large mixing bowl, then add the coconut and make a well in the centre. Melt the butter and sugar in a small saucepan over low heat, stirring until the sugar has dissolved. Remove from the heat. Whisk the combined egg and apricot nectar into the sour cream. Add both the butter and the egg mixtures to the well in the dry ingredients and stir with a wooden spoon until combined.

Divide the mixture evenly among the cases and place an apricot half, cut side up, on the top of each cake. Bake for 18–20 minutes, or until a skewer comes out clean when inserted into the centre of a cake. Transfer onto a wire rack to cool.

Heat the jam in a small saucepan until melted. Brush a little jam over each cake.

# Butterfly cupcakes

**MAKES 12**

120 g (4¼ oz) unsalted butter, softened
145 g (5 oz/⅔ cup) caster (superfine) sugar
185 g (6½ oz/1½ cups) self-raising flour
125 ml (4 fl oz/½ cup) milk
2 eggs
125 ml (4 fl oz/½ cup) thick
(double/heavy) cream
80 g (1½ oz/¼ cup) strawberry jam
icing (confectioners') sugar, to sprinkle

Preheat the oven to 180°C (350°F/Gas 4).
Line 12 standard muffin holes with paper cases.

Beat the butter, sugar, flour, milk and eggs with electric beaters on low speed until combined. Increase to medium speed and beat until the mixture is smooth and pale.

Divide the mixture evenly among the cases and bake for 15–20 minutes, or until a skewer comes out clean when inserted into the centre of a cake. Transfer onto a wire rack to cool.

Cut a shallow round from the centre of each cake using the point of a sharp knife, then cut the round in half. Spoon 2 teaspoons of cream into the cavity of each cake, then top with 1 teaspoon of jam. Position the two halves of the cake round in the jam to resemble butterfly wings. Sprinkle with sifted icing sugar.

# Peanut butter mini cupcakes

**MAKES 18**

150 g (5½ oz) unsalted butter, chopped
115 g (4 oz/½ cup) soft brown sugar
2 eggs
125 g (4½ oz/½ cup) crunchy peanut butter
125 g (4½ oz/1 cup) self-raising flour
30 g (1 oz/¼ cup) plain (all-purpose) flour
60 ml (2 fl oz/¼ cup) milk

**Hazelnut and peanut butter icing (frosting)**
120 g (4¼ oz/½ cup) hazelnut spread, softened
90 g (3¼ oz/⅓ cup) crunchy peanut butter,
  softened
2 x 60 g (2¼ oz) chocolate-coated peanut bars
  (such as Snickers), chopped

Preheat the oven to 180°C (350°F/Gas 4).
Line 18 flat-bottomed patty holes with paper cases.

Beat the butter and sugar together in a bowl with
electric beaters until light and creamy. Add the eggs,
one at a time, beating well after each addition. Add
the peanut butter and beat until combined. Fold in the
sifted flours alternately with the milk until combined.

Divide the mixture evenly among the cases. Bake for
10–12 minutes, or until a skewer comes out clean
when inserted into the centre of a cake. Transfer onto
a wire rack to cool completely.

To make the hazelnut and peanut butter icing,
combine the hazelnut spread and peanut butter.
Spread the icing over each cake and decorate with
a piece of chocolate peanut bar.

# Jam doughnut cupcakes

**MAKES 18**

155 g (5½ oz/1¼ cups) self-raising flour
115 g (4 oz/½ cup) caster (superfine) sugar
125 ml (4 fl oz/½ cup) milk
2 eggs
1 teaspoon natural vanilla extract
½ teaspoon dried yeast
160 g (5⅔ oz/½ cup) strawberry jam
20 g (¾ oz) unsalted butter, melted
2 tablespoons cinnamon sugar

Preheat the oven to 180°C (350°F/Gas 4).
Line 18 standard muffin holes with paper cases.

Combine the flour and sugar in a bowl, and make a
well in the centre. Put the milk, eggs, vanilla and
yeast in a jug and whisk to combine. Pour into the
well in dry ingredients and whisk until smooth.

Divide half the mixture evenly among the cases.
Top each with 1 teaspoon of jam, then cover with the
remaining mixture. Bake for 10–12 minutes, or until
a skewer comes out clean when inserted into the
centre of a cake. Brush a little melted butter over
each cake, then dip it into the cinnamon sugar.
Serve the cakes warm.

# Honey, banana and macadamia cupcakes

**MAKES 32**

Preheat the oven to 180°C (350°F/Gas 4). Line 32 mini muffin holes with paper cases.

Melt the butter and honey in a small saucepan, stirring until combined. Allow to cool.

Sift the flour and mixed spice into a large bowl. Add the carrot, banana, macadamias, eggs and honey mixture, stirring until the mixture is just combined and smooth.

Divide the mixture evenly among the cases, and sprinkle the tops liberally with extra chopped macadamias. Bake for 8 minutes, or until a skewer comes out clean when inserted into the centre of a cake. Transfer onto a wire rack to cool.

Drizzle a little honey over the cakes before serving.

100 g (3½ oz) unsalted butter, chopped
350 g (12 oz/1 cup) honey, plus extra to drizzle
250 g (9 oz/2 cups) self-raising flour
1 teaspoon mixed spice
150 g (5½ oz/1½ cups) coarsely grated carrot
1 ripe banana, mashed
70 g (2½ oz/½ cup) chopped macadamia nuts, plus extra, to sprinkle
2 eggs, lightly beaten

# Neenish cupcakes

**MAKES 16**

250 g (9 oz) unsalted butter
230 g (8½ oz/1 cup) caster (superfine) sugar
1 teaspoon natural vanilla extract
4 eggs
185 g (6½ oz/1½ cups) self-raising flour, sifted
60 g (2¼ oz/½ cup) plain (all-purpose) flour, sifted
185 ml (6 fl oz/¾ cup) milk
30 g (1 oz/¼ cup) unsweetened cocoa powder, sifted

**Icing (frosting)**
185 g (6½ oz/1½ cups) icing (confectioners') sugar, sifted
10 g (¼ oz) unsalted butter

**Chocolate topping**
200 g (7 oz) dark chocolate, roughly chopped

Preheat the oven to 180°C (350°F/Gas 4). Line 16 standard muffin holes with paper cases.

Beat the butter, sugar and vanilla together with electric beaters until light and creamy. Add the eggs, one at a time, beating well after each addition. Fold in the flours alternately with the milk. Divide the mixture in half and stir the cocoa through one half of the mixture until well combined. Divide the chocolate mixture evenly into half of the cases. Then divide the plain mixture into the other half, so that each case is filled with half chocolate and half plain mixtures. Bake for 18–20 minutes, or until a skewer comes out clean when inserted into the centre of a cake. Transfer onto a wire rack to cool.

To make the white icing, place the icing sugar and butter in a small heatproof bowl. Stir in enough warm water to form a smooth paste. Sit the bowl over a small saucepan of simmering water and stir until smooth and glossy. Remove from the heat. Spread the icing over the white side of each cake.

To make the chocolate topping, place the chocolate in a small bowl over a saucepan of simmering water, and stir occasionally until the chocolate has melted. Spread the chocolate over the other half of the cakes.

# Apple pecan cupcakes

**MAKES 16**

Preheat the oven to 180°C (350°F/Gas 4). Line 16 standard muffin holes with paper cases.

Combine the flour, cinnamon, sugar, apple and pecans in a bowl. Add the egg, milk and melted butter, stirring until the mixture is just combined and smooth.

Divide the mixture evenly among the cases. Bake for 18–20 minutes, or until a skewer comes out clean when inserted into the centre of a cake. Transfer onto a wire rack to cool.

If desired, sprinkle with icing sugar and serve with thick cream or yoghurt.

310 g (11 oz/2½ cups) self-raising flour
1½ teaspoons ground cinnamon
165 g (5¾ oz/¾ cup) caster (superfine) sugar
2 granny smith's apples (about 340 g/11¾ oz), peeled, cored and coarsely grated
50 g (1¾ oz/½ cup) pecans, chopped
2 eggs, lightly beaten
125 ml (4 fl oz/½ cup) milk
15 g (½ oz) unsalted butter, melted
thick (double/heavy) cream or yoghurt, to serve (optional)

# Beehive cupcakes

200 g (7 oz) unsalted butter, softened
185 g (6½ oz/1 cup) soft brown sugar
3 eggs
115 g (4 oz/⅓ cup) honey, warmed
280 g (10 oz/2¼ cups) self-raising flour, sifted

**Marshmallow icing (frosting)**
3 egg whites
330 g (11¾ oz/1½ cups) sugar
2 teaspoons light corn syrup
pinch of cream of tartar
1 teaspoon natural vanilla extract
yellow food colouring
15 toothpicks
15 chocolate-foil wrapped bumble bees
with wings

Preheat the oven 180°C (350°F/Gas 4). Line 15 standard muffin holes with paper cases.

Beat the butter and sugar with electric beaters until light and creamy. Add the eggs, one at a time, beating well after each addition. Fold in the honey and flour until combined. Divide the mixture evenly among the cases. Bake for 18–20 minutes, or until a skewer comes out clean when inserted into the centre of a cake. Transfer onto a wire rack to cool.

To make the marshmallow icing, combine the egg whites, sugar, corn syrup, cream of tartar and 100 ml (3½ fl oz) of water in a heatproof bowl. Sit the bowl over a saucepan of simmering water, making sure the bowl doesn't touch the water. Beat for 5 minutes with electric beaters, or until the mixture is light and fluffy. Remove from the heat. Add the vanilla and beat with electric beaters for 4–5 minutes, or until stiff peaks form. Add the colouring, drop by drop, and beat until just combined.

Spoon the icing into a piping bag fitted with a 1 cm (½ inch) round nozzle, and pipe the icing in circles around the cake to resemble a beehive. Push the pointy end of the toothpick into the base of each bee and insert it into each cake.

# Mini pear and walnut cupcakes

**MAKES 36**

150 g (5½ oz) unsalted butter, softened
140 g (5 oz/¾ cup) soft brown sugar
2 eggs
155 g (5½ oz/1¼ cups) self-raising flour, sifted
125 ml (4 fl oz/½ cup) milk
135 g (3½ oz/½ cup) tinned pears, well drained and chopped
40 g (1½ oz/⅓ cup) chopped walnuts

**Maple cream icing (frosting)**
90 g (3¼ oz) cream cheese, softened
60 ml (2 fl oz/¼ cup) maple syrup
185 g (6½ oz/1½ cups) icing (confectioners') sugar, sifted
60 g (2¼ oz/½ cup) chopped walnuts, to decorate

Preheat the oven to 180°C (350°F/Gas 4). Line 36 mini muffin holes with paper cases.

Beat the butter and sugar together with electric beaters until light and creamy. Add the eggs, one at a time, beating well after each addition. Fold in the flour alternately with the milk. Fold in the pears and the walnuts. Divide the mixture evenly among the cases. Bake for 12–15 minutes, or until a skewer comes out clean when inserted into the centre of a cake. Transfer onto a wire rack to cool.

To make the maple cream icing, beat the cream cheese and maple syrup with electric beaters until combined. Gradually beat in the icing sugar until combined. Spread the icing over each cake and decorate with chopped walnuts.

# Milk chocolate buttons

**MAKES 12**

75 g (2½ oz) unsalted butter
75 g (2½ oz) milk chocolate, chopped
80 g (2¾ oz/⅓ cup) soft brown sugar
2 eggs, lightly beaten
60 g (2¼ oz/½ cup) self-raising flour, sifted

**Ganache**
80 g (2¾ oz) milk chocolate, chopped
2 tablespoons thick (double/heavy) cream
silver cachous, to decorate

Preheat the oven to 160°C (315°F/Gas 2–3).
Line 12 mini muffin holes with paper cases.

Place the butter and chocolate in a heatproof bowl and
sit the bowl over a saucepan of simmering water,
making sure the bowl doesn't touch the water. Stir the
chocolate until melted. Remove the bowl from the heat
and mix in the sugar and egg. Stir in the flour.

Transfer the mixture to a jug and pour evenly among
the cases. Bake for 20–25 minutes, or until cooked.
Leave in the tin for 10 minutes, then transfer onto a
wire rack to cool completely.

To make the ganache, place the chocolate and cream
in a heatproof bowl. Sit the bowl over a saucepan
of simmering water, making sure the bowl
doesn't touch the water. Once the chocolate has
almost melted, remove the bowl from the heat and
stir until the remaining chocolate has melted and the
mixture is smooth. Allow to cool for about 8 minutes,
or until thickened slightly.

Return the cakes to the cold tin to keep them stable
while you spread 1 heaped teaspoon of ganache over
each cake. Decorate with silver cachous.

# Banana sour cream cupcakes

**MAKES 24**

185 g (6½ oz) unsalted butter, softened
230 g (8½ oz/1 cup) caster (superfine) sugar
3 eggs
310 g (11 oz/2½ cups) self-raising flour
½ teaspoon bicarbonate of soda (baking soda)
185 g (6½ oz/¾ cup) sour cream
2 tablespoons maple syrup
3 very ripe bananas, mashed (about 300 g/10½ oz)

**Honey cream icing (frosting)**
80 g (2¾ oz) cream cheese, softened
50 g (1¾ oz) unsalted butter, softened
1½ tablespoons honey
250 g (9 oz/2 cups) icing (confectioners')
sugar, sifted

Preheat the oven to 180°C (350°F/Gas 4).
Line 24 standard muffin holes with paper cases.

Beat the butter and sugar in a large bowl using electric beaters for 5–6 minutes, or until light and fluffy. Add the eggs, one at a time, beating well after each addition.

Sift the flour and bicarbonate of soda together. Add the sour cream and maple syrup to the mashed banana and mix well. Fold the flour mixture alternately with the banana mixture in the butter mixture until well combined.

Divide the mixture evenly among the cases. Bake for 15 minutes, or until a skewer comes out clean when inserted into the centre of a cake. Transfer onto a wire rack to cool.

To make the honey cream icing, place the cream cheese and butter in a small bowl and beat with electric beaters until smooth. Add the honey and icing sugar and beat until smooth and well combined. Decorate each cake generously with the icing.

# Marble patty cakes

MAKES 10

185 g (6½ oz) unsalted butter, softened
170 g (6 oz/¾ cup) caster (superfine) sugar
1 teaspoon natural vanilla extract
3 eggs
125 g (4½ oz/1 cup) self-raising flour
30 g (1 oz/¼ cup) plain (all-purpose) flour
125 ml (4 fl oz/½ cup) milk
pink food colouring
2 tablespoons unsweetened cocoa
   powder, sifted

**Marble icing (frosting)**
280 g (10 oz/2¼ cups) icing (confectioners')
   sugar, sifted
100 g (3½ oz) unsalted butter, softened
pink food colouring

Preheat the oven to 180°C (350°F/Gas 4).
Line 10 standard muffin holes with paper cases.

Beat the butter, sugar and vanilla together with electric beaters until light and creamy. Add the eggs, one at a time, beating well after each addition. Sift the flours together and fold in alternately with the milk.

Divide the mixture into three equal portions. Add a few drops of pink food colouring to one portion and mix to combine. Add the cocoa to another portion and mix to combine. Divide the three colours evenly into each case and gently swirl the mixture with a skewer. Bake for 15 minutes, or until a skewer comes out clean when inserted into the centre of a cake. Transfer onto a wire rack to cool.

To make the marble icing, mix the icing sugar, butter and enough hot water to make a spreadable icing. Spread the icing over each cake. Dip a skewer in pink food colouring and swirl it through the icing to create a marbled effect.

# Pecan and orange cupcakes

### MAKES 16 or 24 mini

125 g (4½ oz) unsalted butter, softened
170 g (6 oz/¾ cup) caster (superfine) sugar
2 eggs
100 g (3½ oz/¾ cup) ground pecans
3 teaspoons finely grated orange zest
185 g (6½ oz/1½ cups) self-raising flour, sifted
125 ml (4 fl oz/½ cup) milk

### Cinnamon icing (frosting)
15 g (½ oz) unsalted butter, softened
¾ teaspoon ground cinnamon
185 g (6½ oz/1½ cups) icing (confectioners')
sugar, sifted

Preheat the oven to 180°C (350°F/Gas 4). Line 16 standard (or 24 mini) muffin holes with paper cases.

Beat the butter and sugar with electric beaters until pale and creamy. Gradually add the eggs, one at a time, beating well after each addition. Add the ground pecans and orange zest, then use a metal spoon to gently fold in the flour alternately with the milk.

Divide the mixture evenly among the cases. Bake for 50–60 minutes (40 minutes for minis), or until a skewer comes out clean when inserted into the centre of a cake. Leave in the tin for 10 minutes, then transfer onto a wire rack to cool.

To make the cinnamon icing, combine the butter, icing sugar and cinnamon in a small bowl with 1½ tablespoons of hot water. Sit the bowl over a saucepan of simmering water, making sure the bowl doesn't touch the water, and stir until smooth and glossy. Remove from the heat. Decorate each cake with icing.

# White chocolate chip cupcakes

**MAKES 12**

125 g (4½ oz) unsalted butter, softened
170 g (6 oz/¾ cup) caster (superfine) sugar
2 eggs
1 teaspoon natural vanilla extract
250 g (9 oz/2 cups) self-raising flour, sifted
125 ml (4 fl oz/½ cup) buttermilk
200 g (7 oz/1¼ cups) white chocolate chips

Preheat the oven to 170°C (325°F/Gas 3). Line 12 standard muffing holes with paper cases.

Beat the butter and sugar in a large bowl with electric beaters until pale and creamy. Gradually add the eggs, one at a time, beating well after each addition. Add the vanilla extract and beat until combined. Fold in the flour alternately with the buttermilk, then fold in the chocolate chips.

Divide the mixture evenly among the cases until three-quarters full. Bake for 20 minutes, or until a skewer comes out clean when inserted into the centre of a cake. Leave the cakes in the tin for 5 minutes, then transfer onto a wire rack to cool.

# Rhubarb yoghurt cupcakes

**MAKES 24**

150 g (5½ oz/1½ cups) finely sliced fresh
rhubarb, plus 24 extra pieces to garnish
310 g (11 oz/2½ cups) self-raising flour, sifted
230 g (8½ oz/1 cup) caster (superfine) sugar
1 teaspoon natural vanilla extract
2 eggs, lightly beaten
125 g (4½ oz/½ cup) plain yoghurt
1 tablespoon rosewater
125 g (4½ oz) unsalted butter, melted

Preheat the oven to 180°C (350°F/Gas 4).
Line 24 standard muffin holes with paper cases.

Combine the rhubarb, flour and sugar in a bowl. Add
the vanilla, egg, yoghurt, rosewater and the melted
butter, stirring with a wooden spoon until the mixture
is just combined.

Divide the mixture evenly among the cases, then top
with a piece of rhubarb. Bake for 15 minutes, or until
a skewer comes out clean when inserted into the
centre of a cake. Transfer onto a wire rack to cool.

# Apple and raisin cupcakes

**MAKES 12**

185 g (6½ oz/1½ cups) self-raising flour
150 g (5½ oz) unsalted butter, chopped
140 g (5 oz/¾ cup) soft brown sugar
125 g (4½ oz/1 cup) raisins, plus extra
  to garnish
120 g (4¼ oz) apple purée
3 eggs, lightly beaten

**Yoghurt topping**
250 g (9 oz/1 cup) plain yoghurt
1 tablespoon soft brown sugar

Preheat the oven to 180°C (350°F/Gas 4).
Line 12 standard muffin holes with paper cases.

Sift the flour into a large bowl and make a well in the centre. Melt the butter and sugar in a small saucepan over a low heat, stirring until the sugar has dissolved. Remove from the heat. Combine the raisins and apple purée with the butter mixture. Pour into the well in the flour, along with the egg. Stir with a wooden spoon until combined.

Divide the mixture evenly among the cases. Bake for 15 minutes, or until a skewer comes out clean when inserted into the centre of a cake. Transfer onto a wire rack to cool completely.

To make the yoghurt topping, combine the yoghurt and sugar. Spread 1 tablespoon of topping over each cake.

# Long afternoon teas

These elegant offerings call for an aromatic brew
to be sipped slowly from your finest china cup.

# Pistachio and cardamom cupcakes

**MAKES 24**

140 g (5 oz/1 cup) unsalted pistachio kernels
½ teaspoon ground cardamom, plus extra
to sprinkle
150 g (5½ oz) unsalted butter, chopped
185 g (6½ oz/1½ cups) self-raising flour
170 g (6 oz/¾ cup) caster (superfine) sugar
3 eggs
125 g (½ oz/½ cup) plain yoghurt

**Lime syrup**
115 g (4 oz/½ cup) caster (superfine) sugar
rind of 1 lime, white pith removed

**Honey yoghurt topping**
250 g (9 oz/1 cup) plain yoghurt
1 tablespoon honey

Preheat the oven to 180°C (350°F/Gas 4). Line 24 standard muffin holes with paper cases.

Place the pistachios and cardamom in a food processor and pulse until just chopped. Add the butter, flour and caster sugar and pulse for 20 seconds, or until crumbly. Add the eggs and yoghurt and pulse until just combined.

Divide the mixture evenly among the cases. Bake for 15 minutes, or until a skewer comes out clean when inserted into the centre of a cake. Transfer onto a wire rack to cool.

To make the lime syrup, place the caster sugar and 100 ml (3½ fl oz) of water in a small saucepan and stir over low heat until the sugar has dissolved. Bring to the boil, then add the rind and cook for 5 minutes. Strain. Brush the syrup over the cakes while they're still warm, and then allow to cool.

To make the honey yoghurt topping, place the yoghurt and honey in a small bowl and stir until well combined. Decorate each cake with the honey yoghurt and a sprinkle of ground cardamom.

# Fruit tart cupcakes

**MAKES 12**

Preheat the oven to 180°C (350°F/Gas 4). Line 12 standard muffin holes with paper cases.

Beat the butter, sugar and vanilla together with electric beaters until light and creamy. Add the eggs, one at a time, beating well after each addition. Sift the flours together and fold in alternately with the milk.

Divide the mixture evenly among the cases. Bake for 15 minutes, or until a skewer comes out clean when inserted into the centre of a cake. Transfer onto a wire rack to cool.

Cut the centre out of each cake, leaving a 1 cm (½ inch) border. Fill each cavity with 2 teaspoons of custard. Cut the fruit and arrange over the custard. Heat the jam until runny. Lightly brush the jam over the top of each cake. Refrigerate until ready to serve.

185 g (6½ oz) unsalted butter, softened
170 g (6 oz/¾ cup) caster (superfine) sugar
1 teaspoon natural vanilla extract
3 eggs
125 g (4½ oz/1 cup) self-raising flour
30 g (1 oz/¼ cup) plain (all-purpose) flour
125 ml (4 fl oz/½ cup) milk
125 g (4½ oz/½ cup) thick custard
1 kiwi fruit, peeled
125 g (4½ oz) strawberries
1 freestone peach, peeled
red grapes (about 4 to 6)
160 g (5⅔ oz/½ cup) apricot jam

# Chocolate and almond cupcakes

**MAKES 36**

100 g (3½ oz) dark chocolate, chopped
50 g (1¾ oz/½ cup) ground almonds
90 g (3¼ oz/¾ cup) self-raising flour
4 eggs, separated
115 g (4 oz/½ cup) caster (superfine) sugar
2 tablespoons warm milk
chocolate flakes, to decorate
unsweetened cocoa powder, to sprinkle

**Chocolate ganache**
100 g (3½ oz) dark chocolate, chopped
100 g (3½ oz) unsalted butter

Preheat the oven to 180°C (350°F/Gas 4). Line 36 mini muffin holes with paper cases.

Place the chocolate in a food processor and process until finely ground. Add the ground almonds and flour and process until just combined.

Beat the egg yolks and sugar with electric beaters for 2–3 minutes, or until thick and pale. Stir in the chocolate mixture, then the milk. Beat the egg whites in a clean bowl until soft peaks form. Gently fold the whites into the mixture with a metal spoon until just combined. Divide the mixture evenly among the cases. Bake for 10–12 minutes, or until a skewer comes out clean when inserted into the centre of a cake. Transfer onto a wire rack to cool.

To make the chocolate ganache, place the chocolate and butter in a small heatproof bowl over a saucepan of simmering water, making sure the bowl doesn't touch the water. Stir until smooth and combined. Refrigerate for 20 minutes, stirring occasionally until thickened.

Cut the centre out of the cakes. Fill each cavity with 1 teaspoon of chocolate ganache, then decorate with chocolate flakes and cocoa.

# Mandarin and chamomile cupcakes

**MAKES 20**

Preheat the oven to 180°C (350°F/Gas 4). Line 20 mini muffin holes with paper cases.

Place the milk and chamomile tea flowers into a saucepan and bring just to the boil. Stand for 5 minutes to infuse. Strain.

Place the butter, sugar, eggs, mandarin zest and mandarin in a food processor and process until almost smooth. Add the milk mixture, semolina and flour and process until smooth. Pour the mixture evenly among the cases. Bake for 8–10 minutes, or until a skewer comes out clean when inserted into the centre of a cake. Transfer onto a wire rack to cool.

To make the mandarin glaze, place the icing sugar, zest and enough juice to make a paste in a heatproof bowl. Sit the bowl over a saucepan of simmering water, making sure the base of the bowl doesn't touch the water, and stir until runny. Remove from the heat but keep the bowl over the water. Spread the glaze over each cake and decorate with a chamomile flower.

185 ml (6 fl oz/¾ cup) milk
5 g (⅛ oz/¼ cup) chamomile tea flowers, plus extra to decorate
150 g (5½ oz) unsalted butter, chopped
230 g (8½ oz/1 cup) caster (superfine) sugar
3 eggs
2 teaspoons finely grated mandarin zest
300 g (10½ oz) mandarin, peeled, seeds removed
60 g (2¼ oz/½ cup) fine semolina
155 g (5⅔ oz/1¼ cups) self-raising flour

**Mandarin glaze**
155 g (5½ oz/1¼ cups) icing (confectioners') sugar, sifted
1 teaspoon finely grated mandarin zest
2–3 tablespoons strained, fresh mandarin juice
chamomile tea flowers, to garnish

# Individual blueberry cheesecakes

**MAKES 6**

**Cheese mixture**
115 g (4 oz/½ cup) caster (superfine) sugar
85 g (3 oz/⅓ cup) cream cheese

**Blueberry sauce**
250 g (9 oz/1⅔ cups) blueberries
1 tablespoon crème de cassis

165 g (5¾ oz/1⅓ cups) plain (all-purpose) flour
1 tablespoon baking powder
20 g (¾ oz) unsalted butter, melted
1 teaspoon finely grated orange zest
1 egg
125 ml (4 fl oz/½ cup) milk
18 blueberries, extra, for filling
icing (confectioners') sugar, to sprinkle

Preheat the oven to 180°C (350°F/Gas 4). Lightly grease 6 standard muffin holes with butter or oil.

To make the cheese mixture, put half the sugar in a bowl with the cream cheese and mix together well.

To make the blueberry sauce, put the blueberries in a blender or food processor with the liqueur and remaining sugar, and blend until smooth. Strain the mixture through a fine sieve to remove any blueberry seeds. Set the cheese mixture and sauce aside.

Sift the flour and baking powder together in a large bowl and stir in the butter, orange zest and ½ teaspoon of salt. In a separate bowl, beat the egg and milk together, then add to the dry ingredients and mix well until combined.

Divide half the mixture evenly among the holes. Add three of the extra blueberries and 1 teaspoon of cheese mixture in each hole, then top with the remaining batter mixture. Bake for 15 minutes, or until cooked and golden. Transfer onto a wire rack to cool slightly. To serve, put each cheescake on a plate, drizzle with blueberry sauce and sprinkle with icing sugar.

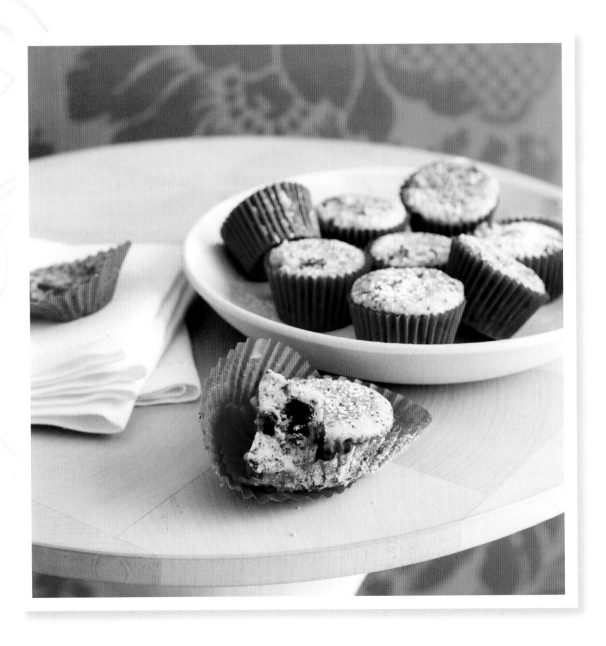

# Prune and ricotta cupcakes

**MAKES 18**

Preheat the oven to 180°C (350°F/Gas 4). Line 18 mini muffin holes with paper cases.

Combine the prunes and Marsala in a small saucepan. Bring to the boil, then reduce the heat and simmer for 30 seconds, or until the Marsala is absorbed. Allow to cool.

Beat the ricotta and sugar with electric beaters for 2 minutes, or until light and creamy. Gradually add the eggs, one at a time, beating well after each addition. Add the cream and beat for 2 minutes. Using a metal spoon, fold in the sifted cornflour and flour, the prune mixture and the chocolate.

Divide the mixture evenly among the cases. Bake for 15–18 minutes, or until firm and lightly golden. Transfer onto a wire rack to cool. Sprinkle with icing sugar just before serving.

75 g (2⅔ oz/⅓ cup) pitted prunes, chopped
1 tablespoon Marsala
250 g (9 oz) ricotta cheese
115 g (4 oz/½ cup) caster (superfine) sugar
2 eggs
60 ml (2 fl oz/¼ cup) whipping cream
30 g (1 oz/¼ cup) cornflour (cornstarch), sifted
2 tablespoons self-raising flour, sifted
30 g (1 oz/¼ cup) grated dark chocolate

65

# Orange and lemon syrup cupcakes

**MAKES 36**

125 g (4½ oz) unsalted butter,
chilled and chopped
230 g (8½ oz/1 cup) caster (superfine) sugar
2 teaspoons finely grated lemon zest
2 teaspoons finely grated orange zest
3 eggs
125 ml (4 fl oz/½ cup) milk
185 g (6½ oz/1½ cups) self-raising flour, sifted

**Lemon syrup**
230 g (8½ oz/1 cup) caster (superfine) sugar
zest of 1 lemon, thinly sliced
zest of 1 orange, thinly sliced

Preheat the oven to 180°C (350°F/Gas 4).
Line 36 mini muffin holes with paper cases.

Place the butter, sugar and lemon and orange zests
in a saucepan and stir over low heat until the sugar
has dissolved. Transfer to a large bowl. Add the eggs,
milk and flour and beat with electric beaters until
just combined.

Divide the mixture evenly among the cases. Bake for
15 minutes, or until a skewer comes out clean when
inserted into the centre of a cake. Transfer onto a wire
rack to cool.

To make the lemon syrup, place 200 ml (7 fl oz) of
water and the sugar in a saucepan over a low heat,
stirring until the sugar has dissolved. Add the lemon
and orange zests, bring to the boil and simmer for
10 minutes, stirring occasionally, or until lightly
golden and syrupy.

Strain the syrup, reserving the zest. Decorate each
cake with some strips of zest and pour over a little
of the syrup.

# Fluffy coconut cupcakes

**MAKES 36**

Preheat the oven to 180°C (350°F/Gas 4). Line 36 mini muffin holes with paper cases.

Combine the flour, coconut and sugar in a bowl and make a well in the centre. Pour in the combined buttermilk, eggs, coconut extract and butter into the well and mix until combined.

Divide the mixture evenly among the cases. Bake for 12 minutes, or until a skewer comes out clean when inserted into the centre of a cake. Transfer onto a wire rack to cool.

To make the coconut icing, combine the icing sugar and coconut in a bowl. Add the butter, coconut extract and enough hot water to make a spreadable icing. Decorate each cake with a thick covering of icing and sprinkle with toasted coconut.

250 g (9 oz/2 cups) self-raising flour, sifted
45 g (1⅔ oz/½ cup) desiccated coconut
230 g (8½ oz/1 cup) caster (superfine) sugar
250 ml (9 fl oz/1 cup) buttermilk
2 eggs, lightly beaten
1 teaspoon natural coconut extract
125 g (4½ oz) unsalted butter, melted

**Coconut icing (frosting)**
280 g (10 oz/2¼ cups) icing (confectioners') sugar
135 g (4¾ oz/1½ cups) desiccated coconut
75 g (2½ oz) unsalted butter, softened
½ teaspoon natural coconut extract
2 tablespoons hot water
desiccated coconut, lightly toasted, to sprinkle

# Hazelnut cream sponge cakes

**MAKES 16**

4 eggs, separated
115 g (4 oz/½ cup) caster (superfine) sugar
60 g (2¼ oz/½ cup) self-raising flour
75 g (2⅔ oz/⅔ cup) ground hazelnuts
20 g (¾ oz) unsalted butter

**Hazelnut icing (frosting)**
170 g (6 oz/½ cup) chocolate hazelnut spread
130 g (4¾ oz) unsalted butter, softened
60 g (2¼ oz/½ cup) icing (confectioners')
sugar, sifted

Preheat the oven to 180°C (350°F/Gas 4). Grease a shallow 20 cm (8 inch) square cake tin and line the base with baking paper.

Beat the egg whites in a clean bowl with electric beaters until soft peaks form. Gradually add the sugar, beating until thick and glossy. Beat the egg yolks into the mixture, one at a time.

Sift the flour over the mixture, add the ground hazelnuts and fold in with a metal spoon. Melt the butter with 2 tablespoons of boiling water in a small bowl, then fold into the sponge mixture. Pour the mixture into the tin and bake for 25 minutes, or until a skewer comes out clean when inserted into the centre of the cake. Leave in the tin for 5 minutes before turning out onto a wire rack to cool. Cut the sponge in half horizontally through the centre.

To make the hazelnut icing, beat the chocolate hazelnut spread and butter with electric beaters until very creamy. Beat in the icing sugar, then gradually add 3 teaspoons of boiling water and beat until smooth. Spread the icing over the base of the sponge, then replace the top layer. Refrigerate until the filling is firm, then cut into squares and place in paper cases.

# Streusel cupcakes

**MAKES 24**

Preheat the oven to 180°C (350°F/Gas 4). Line 24 standard muffin holes with paper cases.

To make the custard, place the egg yolks, sugar and custard powder in a bowl and whisk until pale. Heat the milk in a small saucepan until almost boiling. Remove from the heat, then gradually whisk into the egg mixture. Return the combined mixture to the cleaned saucepan and stir constantly over low heat until the mixture boils and thickens. Refrigerate until cold.

To make the topping, mix all the ingredients together in a bowl, until the mixture resembles coarse breadcrumbs.

Beat the butter, sugar and vanilla together with electric beaters until light and creamy. Add the eggs, one at a time, beating well after each addition. Sift the flours and mixed spice together and fold in alternately with the sultanas and milk. Swirl the custard through the mixture, but do not overmix. Divide the mixture evenly among the cases. Sprinkle the topping over the cakes. Bake for 14–15 minutes, or until a skewer comes out clean when inserted into the centre of a cake. Transfer onto a wire rack to cool.

**Custard**

3 egg yolks
2 tablespoons caster (superfine) sugar
2 tablespoons custard powder
250 ml (9 fl oz/1 cup) milk
1 teaspoon natural vanilla extract

**Topping**

60 g (2¼ oz/½ cup) plain (all-purpose) flour
75 g (2⅔ oz) finely chopped walnuts
95 g (3¼ oz/½ cup) soft brown sugar
80 g (2¾ oz) unsalted butter, melted
1 teaspoon ground cinnamon

185 g (6½ oz) unsalted butter, softened
170 g (6 oz/¾ cup) caster (superfine) sugar
1 teaspoon natural vanilla extract
3 eggs
125 g (4½ oz/1 cup) self-raising flour
30 g (1 oz/¼ cup) plain (all-purpose) flour
1 teaspoon mixed spice
60 g (2¼ oz/½ cup) sultanas (golden raisins)
125 ml (4 fl oz/½ cup) milk

# Passionfruit cupcakes

## MAKES 15

185 g (6½ oz) unsalted butter, softened
170 g (6 oz/¾ cup) caster (superfine) sugar
1 teaspoon natural vanilla extract
3 eggs
125 g (4½ oz) cream cheese, softened
1 tablespoon fresh passionfruit pulp
(1 passionfruit)
125 g (4½ oz/1 cup) self-raising flour
30 g (1 oz/¼ cup) plain (all-purpose) flour
60 ml (2 fl oz/¼ cup) milk

**Passionfruit icing (frosting)**
300 ml (10½ fl oz) whipping cream
1½ tablespoons icing (confectioners') sugar, sifted
2 passionfruit, pulp removed

Preheat the oven to 180°C (350°F/Gas 4).
Line 15 standard muffin holes with paper cases.

Beat the butter, sugar and vanilla together with electric beaters until light and creamy. Add the eggs, one at a time, beating well after each addition. Add the cream cheese and passionfruit and beat until smooth. Sift the flours together and fold in alternately with the milk.

Divide the mixture evenly among the cases. Bake for 15 minutes, or until a skewer comes out clean when inserted into the centre of a cake. Transfer onto a wire rack to cool.

To make the passionfruit icing, beat the cream and icing sugar together until soft peaks form. Cut the centre out of each cake leaving a 1 cm (½ inch) border. Spoon the cream into a piping bag fitted with a 1 cm (½ inch, no 7) star nozzle. Decorate each cake with piped cream and top with the passionfruit.

# Baklava cupcakes

**MAKES 36**

Preheat the oven to 180°C (350°F/Gas 4). Line 36 mini muffin holes with paper cases.

Combine the filling ingredients in a bowl and set aside.

Beat the butter and sugar in a bowl with electric beaters until light and creamy. Add the eggs, one at a time, beating well after each addition. Fold in the sifted flours alternately with the milk, and stir until smooth and combined.

Divide half the mixture evenly among the cases. Sprinkle half the filling over the mixture, then spoon the remaining mixture over the top. Sprinkle over the remaining filling. Bake for 10–12 minutes, or until a skewer comes out clean when inserted into the centre of a cake. Brush warm honey over the cakes while they are still hot.

**Filling**
50 g (1¾ oz) walnuts, chopped
50 g (1¾ oz) blanched almonds, chopped
110 g (3¾ oz/½ cup) raw (demerara) sugar
2 teaspoons ground cinnamon
50 g (1¾ oz) unsalted butter, melted

185 g (6½ oz) unsalted butter, softened
140 g (5 oz/¾ cup) soft brown sugar
3 eggs
125 g (4½ oz/1 cup) self-raising flour
30 g (1 oz/¼ cup) plain (all-purpose) flour
125 ml (4 fl oz/½ cup) buttermilk
90 g (3¼ oz/¼ cup) honey, warmed

79

# Plum and almond cupcakes

MAKES 18

185 g (6½ oz/1½ cups) self-raising flour
1½ teaspoons ground cinnamon
100 g (3½ oz) unsalted butter, melted
230 g (8½ oz/1 cup) soft brown sugar
3 eggs, lightly beaten
50 g (1¾ oz/⅓ cup) blanched almonds, finely chopped
825 g (1 lb 13 oz) tinned stoned plums in natural juice, drained and chopped
dried rose petals, to decorate

**White chocolate cream icing (frosting)**
200 g (7 oz) white chocolate, chopped
125 ml (4 fl oz/½ cup) pouring cream
200 g (7 oz) cream cheese, softened
40 g (2¾ oz/⅓ cup) icing (confectioners') sugar, sifted
pink food colouring

Preheat the oven to 160°C (315°F/Gas 2–3). Line 18 standard muffin holes with paper cases.

Sift the flour and cinnamon together in a bowl. Add the butter, sugar, eggs, almonds and plums and mix with electric beaters until combined.

Divide the mixture evenly among the cases. Bake for 15 minutes, or until a skewer comes out clean when inserted into the centre of a cake. Transfer onto a wire rack to cool.

To make the white chocolate cream icing, combine the chocolate and cream in a small saucepan and stir over low heat until the chocolate has melted. Place the chocolate mixture, cream cheese and icing sugar in a bowl and beat with electric beaters until smooth. Add a few drops of red food colouring and blend evenly. Cover the bowl and refrigerate for 2 minutes, or until slightly firm. Beat the mixture again for a few seconds until smooth.

Spread the icing over each cake and decorate with the dried rose petals.

# Mango cakes with lime syrup

**MAKES 8**

Preheat the oven to 200°C (400°F/Gas 6). Grease 8 large muffin holes, then line with the mango slices.

Beat the butter and sugar in a bowl with electric beaters until light and creamy. Gradually add the eggs, one at a time, beating well after each addition. Fold in the flour, then add the almonds and coconut milk.

Divide the mixture evenly among the holes. Bake for 25 minutes, or until a skewer comes out clean when inserted into the centre of a cake.

To make the lime syrup, place the lime juice, sugar and 125 ml (4 fl oz/½ cup) of water in a small saucepan and stir over low heat until the sugar dissolves. Increase the heat and simmer for 10 minutes.

Pierce holes in each cake with a skewer. Drizzle the syrup over the top and leave for 5 minutes to soak up the liquid. Turn out onto plates and serve.

850 g (1 lb 14 oz) tinned mango slices in syrup, drained
180 g (6½ oz) unsalted butter, softened
120 g (8 oz/1 cup) caster (superfine) sugar
4 eggs
220 g (7¾ oz/1 cup) self-raising flour
4 tablespoons ground almonds
4 tablespoons coconut milk

**Lime syrup**
4 tablespoons lime juice
115 g (4 oz/½ cup) caster (superfine) sugar

# Madeira cupcakes

**MAKES 12**

180 g (6½ oz) unsalted butter, softened
170 g (6 oz/¾ cup) caster (superfine) sugar
3 eggs
165 g (5¾ oz/1⅓ cups) plain (all-purpose) flour
2 teaspoons baking powder
1 teaspoon finely grated orange zest
1 tablespoon orange juice

**Orange icing (frosting)**
250 g (9 oz/2 cups) icing (confectioners')
sugar, sifted
125 g (4½ oz) unsalted butter, softened
1 tablespoon orange juice

Preheat the oven to 180°C (350°/Gas 4).
Line 12 standard muffin holes with paper cases.

Beat the butter and sugar in a bowl, with electric beaters until pale and light. Add the eggs, one at a time, beating well after each addition. Sift the flour and baking powder together. Fold the flour, orange zest and juice into the butter mixture until combined.

Divide the mixture evenly among the cases. Bake for 12–15 minutes, or until a skewer comes out clean when inserted into the centre of a cake. Transfer onto a wire rack to cool completely.

To make the orance icing, place the icing sugar, butter and juice in a large bowl and beat with electric beaters until smooth and well combined. Decorate each cake with icing and sprinkle with icing sugar.

# Chestnut cupcakes

MAKES 36

Preheat the oven to 180°C (350°F/Gas 4). Line 36 mini muffin holes with paper cases.

Beat the butter, sugar and vanilla with electric beaters until light and creamy. Add the chestnut purée and beat for 1 minute, or until just combined. Add the eggs, one at a time, beating well after each addition. Fold in the milk, flour and baking powder, and stir with a wooden spoon until the ingredients are just combined.

Divide the mixture evenly among the cases. Bake for 15 minutes, or until a skewer comes out clean when inserted into the centre of a cake. Transfer onto a wire rack to cool completely.

To make the chocolate glaze, combine the chocolate and cream in a small saucepan. Stir over low heat until the chocolate has melted and the mixture is smooth. Remove from the heat and cool slightly.

Dip the top of each cake into the glaze to coat and decorate each with an icing flower.

125 g (4½ oz) unsalted butter, softened
230 g (8½ oz/1 cup) caster (superfine) sugar
1 teaspoon natural vanilla extract
150 g (5½ oz/½ cup) unsweetened chestnut purée
3 eggs
80 ml (2½ fl oz/⅓ cup) milk
155 g (5⅔ oz/1¼ cups) self-raising flour, sifted
1 teaspoon baking powder
36 flower icing decorations

**Chocolate glaze**
250 g (9 oz) dark chocolate, chopped
185 ml (6 fl oz/¾ cup) pouring cream

# Saffron spice cupcakes

**MAKES 24**

185 ml (6 fl oz/¾ cup) orange juice
3 teaspoons finely grated orange zest
¼ teaspoon saffron threads
2 eggs
125 g (4½ oz/1 cup) icing (confectioners') sugar
1 teaspoon natural vanilla extract
185 g (6½ oz/1½ cups) self-raising flour
155 g (5⅔ oz/1½ cups) ground almonds
100 g (3½ oz) unsalted butter, melted

**Saffron threads**
½ teaspoon saffron threads
2 tablespoons orange juice

**Mascarpone cream**
250 g (9 oz) mascarpone cheese
60 g (2¼ oz/½ cup) icing (confectioners') sugar, sifted
¼ teaspoon ground cardamom

Preheat the oven to 180°C (350°F/Gas 4).
Line 24 standard muffin holes with paper cases.

Combine the orange juice, zest and saffron in a small saucepan and bring to the boil. Reduce the heat and simmer for 1 minute. Leave to cool.

Beat the eggs, icing sugar and vanilla with electric beaters until light and creamy. Fold in the sifted flour, almonds, orange juice mixture and butter with a metal spoon until combined. Divide the mixture evenly among the cases. Bake for 18–20 minutes, or until a skewer comes out clean when inserted into the centre of a cake. Transfer onto a wire rack to cool.

To make the saffron threads, place the saffron and orange juice in a small saucepan and bring to a simmer for 1 minute. Strain and discard the orange juice. Set the saffron threads aside.

To make the mascarpone cream, place the mascarpone, sugar and cardamom in a small bowl and mix to combine (be careful not to overmix or it may curdle). Decorate each cake with piped cream and top with the saffron threads.

# Coconut, ginger and lime cupcakes

**MAKES 36**

150 g (5½ oz) unsalted butter, softened
170 g (6 oz/¾ cup) caster (superfine) sugar
2 teaspoons finely grated lime zest
2 eggs
55 g (2 oz/¼ cup) finely chopped glacé ginger
215 g (7⅔ oz/1¾ cups) self-raising flour
45 g (1⅔ oz/½ cup) desiccated coconut
185 ml (6 fl oz/¾ cup) milk

**Lime icing (frosting)**
125 g (4½ oz/1 cup) icing (confectioners')
   sugar, sifted
10 g (¼ oz) unsalted butter, softened
1 teaspoon finely grated lime zest
2 tablespoons lime juice

Preheat the oven to 180°C (350°F/Gas 4). Line 36 mini muffin holes with paper cases.

Beat the butter, sugar and lime zest with electric beaters until light and creamy. Add the eggs, one at a time, beating well after each addition. Add the ginger. Stir in the sifted flour and the coconut alternately with the milk.

Divide the mixture evenly among the cases. Bake for 15 minutes, or until a skewer comes out clean when inserted into the centre of a cake. Transfer onto a wire rack to cool.

To make the lime icing, combine all of the ingredients, adding enough lime juice to make a smooth, runny icing. Decorate each cake with icing.

# Index

First published in 2008 by Murdoch Books Pty Limited
This edition 2010

Murdoch Books Australia
Pier 8/9
23 Hickson Road
Millers Point NSW 2000
Phone: +61 (0) 2 8220 2000
Fax: +61 (0) 2 8220 2558
www.murdochbooks.com.au

Murdoch Books UK Limited
Erico House, 6th Floor
93–99 Upper Richmond Road
Putney, London SW15 2TG
Phone: +44 (0) 20 8785 5995
Fax: +44 (0) 20 8785 5985
www.murdochbooks.co.uk

Chief Executive: Juliet Rogers
Publishing Director: Kay Scarlett

Commissioning editor: Jane Lawson
Editor: Sandra Davies
Food editor: Chrissy Freer
Design Concept: Reuben Crossman
Design layout: Melanie Ngapo
Cover design: Katy Wall
Photographer: Brett Stevens
Stylist: Lynsey Fryers
Food preparation: Peta Dent
Recipes by: Lee Currie and the Murdoch Books test kitchen
Production: Karen Small

Text, design and photography copyright © 2008
Murdoch Books

National Library of Australia Cataloguing-in-Publication Data
Indulgence cookies / editor, Sandra Davies.
ISBN: 9781741967753
Series: Indulgence series. Includes index.
1. Cupcakes. 641.8653

A catalogue record for this book is available from the
British Library.

PRINTED IN CHINA.

The Publisher and stylist would like to thank Anibou,
Australian Salvage Company, Crowley & Grouch, Domayne
Design, Empire Homewares, Koskela, Miljo, Mokum Textiles
and Tres Fabul for lending equipment for use and
photography.

IMPORTANT: Those who might be at risk from the effects
of salmonella poisoning (the elderly, pregnant women,
young children and those suffering from immune deficiency
diseases) should consult their doctor with any concerns
about eating raw eggs.

OVEN GUIDE: You may find cooking times vary depending
on the oven you are using. For fan-forced ovens, as a general
rule, set the oven temperature to 20°C (35°F) lower than
indicated in the recipe.